The Work And Life Balance Guide

Find Balance Between Your Work And Regular Life Today And Achieve Happiness In The Process

Table of Contents

Introduction

I want to thank you and congratulate you for purchasing *The Work And Life Balance Guide – Find Balance Between Your Work And Regular Life Today And Achieve Happiness In The Process.*

This book contains proven steps and strategies on how to achieve balance between work and personal time, and will serve as your ultimate guide to making sure you enjoy your personal life while seeing to it that you are efficient during office hours.

Learn how to manage your work habits, delegate workload, and draw the line between work and home. Also contained are tips and tricks on how to be passionate about your work and still find time to spend with your friends and loved ones. At the end of this book, you will find that work is no excuse to miss fun and family life. You will learn how to make your job fit into the life that you want.

This book is not only for those trying to find out how to squeeze the fun into their busy schedules but also for people trying to make sense of the stress that they experience at work. This book is also loaded with life hacks to make you more efficient at work and make you realize that you qualify for personal time off.

Thanks again for purchasing this book. I hope you enjoy it!

Chapter 1 - The Problem At Hand

Since the 1970s and the introduction of the concept of overtime, employees like you have been pressured more into spending over 40 hours working every week. You may not notice it, but a lot of offices today are providing the most comfortable sleeping quarters, pantries, and even cots within cubicles. The reason is simple – employers see that more employees are spending overtime to finish work, and it happens that employees tend to sleep inside the office building.

Now the question is, don't these employees miss home?

Don't get it wrong – your employers would actually want you to go home to avoid extra overhead expenses, and you are free to return to your house as long as you get work done. You also have the option of completing office paperwork in your private office, and it is fine that you do work there as long as you stay attached to your phone and your laptop. You are free to go home as long as you are willing to sacrifice the afterhours at the local bar, cancel that always-postponed date with your spouse, or put your children to bed early again so you are not disturbed while you finish work.

Is This an Employer-Employee Problem?

While there are many employers who confess to forcing their employees to bring their mobile phones to the bathroom because they provide instructions on an on-call basis, most employees agree that they do not have enough time to do their job during the office hours. They think their workload is overwhelming and their jobs are too demanding. They think they cannot do anything about it and that the management is just being too hard on them.

On the other hand, there are people who think otherwise about their employers. These are the people who love working so much that they are willing to sacrifice their family life for career advancement. They call this willingness "passion," and they are willing to give up their nightlife and eight hours of sleep to personally ensure they finish a ceiling-high pile of paperwork within 24 hours. These employees are the type of people who think they are the only ones who can pull off the job and that their company would be lost without them.

This Can Be a Costly Problem

Whether you extremely love or hate your work, the attitude that you have about spending too much time at work definitely hurts the business you are working in.

In 2012, BOLT, a business liability insurance company, reported that their clients have lost $134 billion due to hours lost in the office and on top of that is the overtime pay that they shell out to ensure employees can get the work done. Other news says businesses are also losing billions of dollars because of absenteeism. Looking at these reports, your employers are losing money whether you are in the office or not.

Businesses are also losing money when their employees feel burnt out because of work. Stress is very damaging to productivity, and it causes absenteeism, and later on, attrition. However, there seems to be no solution for this problem right now. According to research, work-related stress is one of the most common problems for Americans.

So what exactly is the problem here? It appears that no matter what, companies lose money because there is not enough work being done, and even if they have their best and extremely passionate employees available, they cannot protect them from getting sick and having to stay home from work.

The Solution Seems Simple

It looks like employees simply need to manage their time in order for them to be efficient at work and maintain quality personal time. However, no matter how appealing this solution is, millions of Americans find it hard to commit to this remedy.

Today, you are going to be an exception to the rule. You are going to redefine your work goals and habits in order to manage your time wisely and create a work/life balance.

Chapter 2 - Reasons Why People Choose Work Over Life

You may recognize that you cannot live without work, and there is no denying that having a job in this century is very important. Gone are the days where you ask your parents for money, and you like your ability to pay the bills. However, it is easy for every 21st century employee to feel lost in his work hours, and simply lose the ability to enjoy the little things in life.

Yet, many people stay in their jobs or jump from one to another because they do not want to go back to the purgatory of having to fear their monthly bills. There are also people who have chosen to admit that without their jobs, they do not know what they would be doing. There are also some who think their job description defines them. For those who are raising a family, they are willing to spend a lot of time at work, since it would be for their family's sake.

The Real Reasons Why People Neglect Life

America might be the land of dreams, but it is also the most overworked country in the world. One of the main reasons why many choose work over life in highly industrialized countries is that people tend to think that they can have it all – great paycheck, luxury cars, and a grand house for their family – as long as they commit to their job.

Joanne Ciulla, author of *Working Life: The Promise and Betrayal of Modern Work,* said in an interview that people tend to look at work as the source of their identity and that they have been driven by their desires to earn so that they can purchase security and leisure for them and their families. Soon enough, their commitment to their desire to be rich and to have a comfortable life soon makes them victims of advertising and achieving the allegedly ideal life. You are led to believe that work/life balance is just a myth, and there is nothing that a good job description and a great paycheck will not buy.

Do you think you are one of the many employees in this country that cling to their jobs in order to feel secure, but in the end, lose time for themselves and the people they love? The next chapter will test how willing you are to sacrifice your personal life for your career.

Chapter 3 - Do You Love Your Work More Than Life?

You are definitely aware that you chose to work so you can enjoy life, and if you are a parent or a spouse, to become a person who brings food to the table. While you may think you are working to improve your quality of life, you may be doing the opposite, thanks to your commitment to work.

How you answer the following will determine if you are actually paying more attention to work, and if you are among the 16 percent of Americans who struggle with achieving work/life balance:

1. You tend to spend more hours at work, and when you get home, you are still doing work.

2. You are attached to your electronic devices, and you feel that if you do not check your emails, you may miss one important update from your boss.

3. After you get work done, your body tells you that you need to go straight to bed.

4. Your home is full of stuff from the office.

5. You tend to brush off invitations from your friends and say that you are either at work or too tired to go out.

6. Being able to go home to your family four times a week is considered quality time spent with them.

7. You tend to disappoint romantic partners or your family because of your time spent at work.

8. You seldom use your vacation leaves.

9. You feel overwhelmed at work, and you find yourself committing to too many things.

10. You think about work when you are not working.

11. You are unsure about what your hobbies are and what you do for leisure.

12. You tend to feel lethargic, even though the workweek has just barely started.

13. You often feel anxious or frustrated because of work.

14. You feel guilty because you barely have time to do the things you like to do.

15. You think about work even after office hours, and you think about what you should do the next time you are in the office.

16. You feel that you cannot do anything leisurely or something for yourself even once a week.

17. You miss important family events because you feel that you need to work.

18. You work through your breaks.

19. You feel that you have little or no control over your job.

If this list describes your life, then you definitely need to work on your work/life balance. You need to address the lack of balance in order for you to ensure that you do not become burnt out due to work-related stress.

Why Is This a Problem?

If you think that your commitment to your job is too much (to the point that it hurts), then you may not be getting the things you want out of your job. When the stress is too much to handle, you will feel less motivated to accomplish tasks, and eventually, you will reach the boiling point of dreading work. At the same time, you might be letting your relationships and your health suffer, leaving you less buffer to actually deal with stress.

The ability to handle work-related stress almost always comes from your personal life. It gives you the opportunity to see that while doing your job can be too much hassle at times, you will always find comfort somewhere else. Achieving this balance gives you a breathing room and, at the same time, gives you peace of mind knowing you can enjoy non-work things, such as your house, hobbies, and lifestyle.

The next chapter will tell you how you can identify the root cause of the problem and determine your goals to achieve harmony between your personal life and work.

Chapter 4 - Define Your Goals And Make Life Happen

Having a balance between work and your personal life is not a myth, and you can achieve it as long as you make a commitment to getting more from life. This chapter will help you identify your goals in life and see to it that you are enjoying the time you spend at work and with the people that matter to you. At the same time, you will also find that you actually have time to spend for yourself.

What Do You Want Out of Work?

You probably work hard because you desire the following:

1. Be able to pay your bills on time and see to it that your obligations are met.

2. Develop self-esteem and be considered an important component of the community.

3. Become certain that you can sustain yourself and your family even after retirement.

4. Achieve comfort for you and your loved ones.

5. Find satisfaction in your workplace and continue to build great relationships with the people there.

6. Feel accomplished and established in your career.

7. Improve your skills and learn new ones.

These are the most common goals of any employee you will meet. In general, all employees out there want to be financially stable and feel secure, experience comfort, assert their importance, and make sure their loved ones will reap the rewards of their hard work. In order to achieve these goals, it is important that you assert your needs – you need to enjoy the benefits you should be getting from work.

What You Really Want

Face it – you do not want to spend the entire day working in the office, or having to tend to additional tasks during the afterhours. Any employee wants to achieve the following every day:

1. Be able to tend to personal health needs, such as being able to eat complete meals, without feeling pressure to hurry.

2. Spend time with loved ones and be involved in their lives.

3. Have time for recreation and be able to perform a hobby or an activity of interest.

4. Develop harmonious relationships with others after work.

5. Have the peace of mind that it is possible to take vacations without being made to feel there is too much work to be done upon returning to work.

6. Be able to stick to the hours of the shift and not think about work at home or during days off.

7. Be able to limit the tasks according to one's capacity to work during that day and the time allotted.

8. Achieve motivation from authorities and enjoy healthy pressure in the workplace.

9. Feel that compensation is enough for the amount of work being done within the shift.

The items on this list are basic, and in an ideal world, should be achieved easily. Sadly, most employees feel great stress because of the pressure to work all hours of the day.

What Prevents Balance From Happening?

The easiest way to put it is that you are probably not able to define the line between the different activities that you need and want to do. While you recognize that work is very important to you, you also have to understand that you have your personal needs to attend to as well. The only solution is to set boundaries between life and work and remember that your job exists in order for you to get better things out of life. The next chapter will show you the initial steps you need to take to achieve that.

Chapter 5 - Drawing The Line Between Work And Home

Your home is your sanctuary from all the things outside that contribute stress. For that reason, is very important that you separate work from your home life. In doing so, once you arrive home, you can automatically relax. Here are some tips you can use to achieve this.

1. Do not bring homework.

This is the most crucial step if you want to have a life away from work. As much as possible, do not clutter your home with paperwork from the office. Do not answer your boss' email in the bedroom. Do not bring the company home with you.

2. Make your house feel like home.

Make your home conducive for rest. During weekends, see to it that you are able to tidy up your house and that you replenish your pantry stock. See to it that your house is the place where you hold your simple pleasures, which will help you relax after the long day is done.

3. Indulge in comfortable furniture and homey appliances.

What would make you want to go home as soon as work is done and avoid over time? Make sure your home is fully furnished with all the things that give your body and mind comfort. If your budget allows it, invest in the most comfortable couch you can think of. Make your weekend movie nights worth it by getting a great home entertainment system.

If you are just starting to make money, being comfortable does not need to be expensive. Just make sure you have space at home allotted for personal use. Have a favorite chair or a hobby corner. As long as you can really feel at home in your own house, you will want to hurry home after your shift.

4. Use two computers.

This is something that works for both telecommuters and brick-and-mortar office workers – use two computers. Make sure the computer you are using for work only contain office-related materials, while the other has links to social media accounts, shopping sites, and other personal and entertainment files. This would not only increase productivity but also see to it that you do not unintentionally open office files at home.

5. Do not multitask, especially at home.

Make sure you do not do any activity, either at home or in the office, that would compromise the sanctity of the line you are trying to create. If you want to take care of your home bills, do it at home, or have someone else do it. If you are trying to cook at home, do not attend to your work email while you are waiting for the pasta to be done. The key is to make sure you are doing things one at a time, in the proper venues.

6. If you can't help but do some job-related tasks, make sure that you have an office at home.

You do not have to build another room to have an office inside your home. As long as it is away from most foot traffic and it is conducive for work, then the space is fine. If you are pressed for time and need to bring work home, make sure you complete the work only in the office, not elsewhere. At the same time, make sure that once you leave the office, all your thoughts about work stay there.

Now, you have a solid idea on how you can make sure your home is just for your personal life, and nothing else. The next chapter will show you how you can make sure you keep this boundary by managing your time.

Chapter 6 - Managing Time To Be Able To Do More

After reading the previous chapter, you must be wondering how you can actually commit to coming home and not doing any work there. The key to actually doing that lies in de-cluttering your schedule and finding time to complete work tasks in the office. Make sure you finish every work-related task during your shift. Here are some tips you can use to make this happen:

1. Use time blocking

If your workday is normally swamped with surprise appointments, then it is time to use your planner to schedule all of them ahead of time. Make it your work policy to commit to only one schedule at a time.

2. Again, do not multitask.

You will find that you are more productive and can maintain your train of thought when you are handling one task at a time. You can also avoid progress confusion this way and prevent having to repeat processes all over again because you got lost.

3. Plan your tasks ahead.

In other words, have a to-do list that goes along with your time blocks. Make sure there are no conflicts in your schedule, and see to it that you are going to complete tasks within a given time period using your planner.

4. Break down large and difficult tasks.

If you are assigned a difficult and time-consuming task, it may be wise to think of how you can divide your time so you can handle other tasks as well. You can try dividing tasks into four processes. That way you can monitor your progress and attend to the more difficult segments at a later time.

5. Delegate tasks.

If you believe you cannot handle all assigned tasks on your own, do not succumb to the thought that your boss would be disappointed if you do not single-handedly finish them. It is always more efficient and progressive to ask for someone else's help when needed. Not only can you actually finish work at a much faster pace, you also avoid being overburdened and spreading yourself too thin.

6. Do not waste time on social media.

This may not be a surprise anymore – companies are losing billions of dollars because of the time spent on social media by employees. Reserve logging in to Facebook when you arrive home. This way, you will not need overtime just because you wasted too much time on the Internet.

Following these tips ensures you will save a lot of time and actually finish most, if not all, your tasks during work hours. The next chapter will tell you how to care for your mind and body so it holds up well to work.

Chapter 7 - Have The Right Body And Mind

If you fear Mondays and you feel lethargic when it is barely the middle of the week, your productivity may be suffering. When that happens, you will have a harder time separating work from your personal life.

People who do not have work/life balance are those who suffer the most from ailments caused by work-related stress. If you are looking for the best way to start building relationships, decrease stress, be able to cope with the pressures of work, and have time for personal enjoyment, it is very important that you take health improvement as your first step. The reason is simple – if you have a healthy body, it follows that you also have a healthy mind.

In order for you to perform better at work and still have the energy to enjoy time for yourself and your loved ones when you get home, you need to have a healthy mindset about your job and a body that can withstand all this activity. Here are some tips you can use to achieve that goal:

1. Have enough sleep.

If you have a hard time getting out of the bed in the morning, then your body may be lacking sleep. You need adequate sleep, especially if you are spending a lot of time commuting to work and you are doing long shifts. Not only does this help you feel less cranky in the morning but it also makes you better focused on your tasks.

2. Eat breakfast.

If you feel like a zombie whenever you step inside the office, then you probably should not restrict your morning diet to just coffee. Always see to it that you have time for a healthy breakfast at home before you go to work. That way, you have the energy to do work during the entire shift and avoid wasting time searching the office pantry for snacks.

3. Use your breaks.

If you think that taking breaks destroys productivity, you are quite wrong. Taking a short break of 10 minutes allows you to refresh your brain and create focus when you are ready to get back to work.

4. Use your sick leaves.

You may think you are being a star employee when you go in even though you are sick, but you are not. Not only does any sickness make you a liability while at work, it also makes you create a negative thought in your head that you cannot rest at home even when you need to. When you have these thoughts too often, it eventually leads to hating your job due to burn out.

5. Exercise.

If you are not a fan of exercising, it is time to love it now. Exercising is a good way to build endurance for long hours and to slim down your body if you have not done so in the past years. At the same time, it will do wonders for your self-esteem in the long run and help you do activities after work.

Having a healthy body and a great attitude toward work helps you perform better at work and helps you keep a healthy mindset. This will help keep you relationships outside of work in good shape too.

The next chapter will show you how it is actually possible for you to create relationships that are not related to work. If you have not been paying attention to your social life lately, the next chapter will show you how you can get back in the loop.

Chapter 8 - Rekindling Your Social Life

Your social life is one of the most compelling reasons why you need to separate work from your personal life. You want to feel valued even when you are outside the office, and your friends are the ones who can help you achieve that.

However, you may feel you do not have a social circle outside if you tend to spend too much time in the office doing work-related activities. If you are experiencing the following lately when you are with your friends, then you may have a social life crisis:

1. You are the last one to know about new romantic relationships, life problems, or happenings.

2. Nobody ever asks for your help, because you are always busy.

3. You feel that something is up with the group, but you do not know what that is.

4. You cannot relate to inside jokes.

5. You feel that everybody has changed, and every detail you knew about them does not apply anymore.

6. You feel left out because they are paying more attention to the new person in the group.

You may have been so busy with work that you do not know what is going on with the lives of the people you value the most. Most workaholics suffer from detachment from their family and peers, and they often resolve their frustration by putting more energy into their job, which only worsens the situation. If you think you are losing your grip on your social circle, it is time to salvage your friendships.

Tips and Tricks to Save Your Social Life

If you feel your friends are living their lives without you, then following these tips will definitely make you part of the inner circle again:

1. Start accepting invites.

If you have been missing out on a lot of events in your friends' lives, start making up to your pals. If the invite falls on a night you know you are free, skip the overtime and go.

2. Block a schedule for your friends.

To avoid missing another birthday or any get-together, ask your friends to set these gatherings in advance, so you can make sure those events will not be in conflict with your schedule. That also gives them a proper explanation of why you missed previous events and provides assurance that you are really going to join them on the next gathering.

3. Host a get-together.

If you feel you badly want to make up for your absences and you want them to know what you have been up to, it would be a good idea to host the gathering for your friends in your own place. That way, they have an idea of what your life looks like now. It would also give them the impression that you are welcoming them to your space.

4. Ask them for a night out.

It would certainly be a pleasant surprise for your friends if you give them the heads up that you suddenly want to see them, and that you can do a random get-together. Go to your favorite bar or play a game in your house like you used to when your life was less hectic.

The point is for you to get out there and make time for your friends. Remember that with or without your job, your peers have been there to support you, and it is very important to return that kindness to them. Not only does this allow you to retain your support system, but it also gives you the chance to rediscover that you have a life outside work.

Now that you know how to patch things up with your friends, make sure you also salvage your family life. The next chapter will show you how.

Chapter 9 - Making Time For Your Family

If you think that you have put work over your family life, then it is very likely that you have passed on a lot of opportunities to be with your family. You might be thinking that missing quality time with your loved ones is justified because:

1. You are working hard for them.

2. You can make it up to them if you make more money.

3. You go home to them anyway.

4. They have to understand you are under pressure at work.

If you feel this way toward your family, you may be making them feel like you are distancing yourself. No matter how hard you try to explain to them that you are putting more hours at work so that they can live a more comfortable life, you also need to show them you care in other ways. You do that by being physically, mentally, and emotionally present.

Remember that disappointing your family because you missed birthday parties, holidays and PTA meetings is never worth it. Your loved ones never asked you to sacrifice your time for them.

If you think you have been missing out too much on your loved ones' lives, here are the things you can do to make it up to them and put family time back in your priorities.

1. Watch less television.

If you make it a point to see your favorite game when you are at home but neglect to help out with your kid's homework, then you may want to rearrange your priorities. Cut back on your time with the TV and pay more attention to your family's needs.

2. Ask what they have done during the day.

If you are the type of spouse or parent that seldom talks to your family, start showing them that you are still interested in their lives. The best way to break the ice is to ask them how their day was. That way, you can get to know the people they interact with and how they are doing when you are at work.

3. Get away for the weekend with them.

Yes, you need to take a vacation and guarantee them that you will not think about work when you are with them. That way, you show your family that spending quality time with them is the best relaxation you can give yourself and that they are still number one on your list.

4. Go out on a date with your family members.

If you can take an extended lunch break, it may be a good idea to spend that with a member of the family. Once in a while, call them and ask them to grab a bite with you during workdays. It would also be good recourse if you think you need to spend overtime in the office.

5. Give them a call once in a while.

It would not hurt your schedule to squeeze in a phone call or two to your spouse or your kids when you are on a break. Doing so tells them that they are still on your mind even though you are busy at work.

6. Start work early.

It may be a good idea to ask your employer if it is possible for you to go to work early so you can get out of work in time for dinner. Shifting your schedule an hour earlier than usual may help you create longer quality time with your family. It may also help you avoid heavy traffic.

7. Limit your online time at home.

You can also cut back on the time you spend telling Facebook what happened during the day. If you want to talk about that insane lunch lady or the bad coffee you had, then talk about it with your family instead. They are more interested in your story than Facebook is anyway.

8. Shop with your family.

If you are not the type of person who likes the outdoors and you need to catch up with some errands, take your family out to shop. This is not only the perfect opportunity to shop for groceries, but you will also find out what brands and items they prefer. That way, you can have a better idea what to give them for their birthdays or during the holidays.

9. Organize a game night.

Games are not only great to get to know people in the office, but also to understand the dynamics within your home. It also fosters the idea that your home can still be fun, even though you spend long hours at work.

10. Do a hobby with your loved ones.

If your son is into computer games or your spouse is into working out, indulge them once in a while and be their hobby buddy. Not only does that strengthen your relationship with them and you will know their interests better, it may also give you a nice distraction from work-related stress.

Now that you have a better idea on how to strengthen your ties with the family, it is time to discover how to create time to indulge in your personal comforts. The next chapter will tell you how.

Chapter 10 - Cash In That Vacation

Did you know that 65 percent of working Americans were not able to take their vacation in 2010, and the reason they chose to do that is because they want to look like they work harder? However, you already know that most Americans are not really spending most of the time at their desks on work. This means that not taking your vacation so your boss values you more is not a valid argument at all.

In fact, taking vacations increases your productivity, which may make you a better employee than those who want to be chained to their desks. When you think about it, taking vacations might give you a better shot at the promotion you want. Here are the reasons why:

1. You always find inspiration outside the office.

The office is not built to be a place that inspires. On the other hand, vacations are full of beauty and new perspective, so there is a better chance that your creativity will kick in when you get back to work. That is also the reason why companies nowadays are willing to compensate their top employees with paid vacations – that means they want them to be better focused at work and be more productive.

2. Vacations make you leave your comfort zone.

If you want to prove your leadership skills, then it is very important to let the rest of the team know you are capable of leaving some of the work into their hands. Not only do vacations do wonders for your sanity, they also provide the perfect opportunity for you to test out the effectiveness of your delegation.

Try this: only leave emergency contact procedures to your team and make it a point that they are not to contact you because you trust them well enough. You will see that they are actually very capable of finishing their tasks without you breathing down their necks. It also proves the point that you are organized and that you are able to make everybody work even when you are not there.

3. Vacations provide opportunities for networking.

If you are on sales or marketing or you are actually scouting for a new workplace with a better environment, then taking a vacation may provide you the opportunities you are looking for. Vacations are great for creating new leads, discovering market insights, or looking at other business models without you being too stressed to actually study them. The good part is that they just happen naturally, and you are able to gain without it feeling like work.

4. Vacations help refresh your mind.

It is good to shut off your mind from time to time, and vacations are all about that. Keep in mind that your brain can only take so much, and without giving it a break, you cannot absorb new information, which can be a big problem when you are trying to get promoted. Therefore, if you are eyeing a promotion and you know it requires another level of learning, then give your brain some time off.

If you know you are close to feeling burnt out and you are not sure why, then it is very important to tell your boss that you need to take a leave so you can figure your state. Employers often understand that employees take breaks not only to reward themselves but also to settle internal disputes or just to take a breather. If you ever wonder why CEOs take a lot of vacations, it is because of the amount of decision-making that they are required to make in a day, which means they deal with a lot of stress. Higher-ups that always find something wrong with people are the ones who almost never leave the office.

5. Your vacation leaves will prevent you from using sick leaves.

It is always better not to go to work because you are on a vacation than because you are sick. Vacations are proven to be the employee's best prevention from high blood pressure and increased risk of cardiac arrest. It also helps prevent migraines, flu and colds. In other words, it helps you minimize your trips to the clinic when you are back at work and also help you become a more efficient worker when you are in the office.

Vacations are not only wonderful in making you a better worker, but they also help you reduce all the stress that piles up because of all the years you spent at work without ever taking your leaves. At the same time, it is also the perfect opportunity to help you build better relationships with your friends and loved ones and do activities that you have not done in a long while since you were too busy at work.

Try to forget the old adage that says you are a dedicated employee if you spend more hours at work. By cashing in your vacations, you are able to see to it that your mind and body are always rejuvenated and that you enable yourself to be more efficient in the office. At the same time, having these extended breaks also allows you to make your bosses and teammates realize how integral you are to the company.

Vacations and Quality Time With People and Yourself

Vacations are wonderful because they provide the perfect opportunity for you to find time to be away from the hustle and bustle of the workweek and spend the day with the people that matter the most. They are also a great time for self-reflection.

Vacations also give you a solid reason to not feel required to think about work or guilty about not being there in the office. It is a valid reason to be away from the office and refuse calls, unless it is an emergency.

These extended work timeouts are also useful in determining whether you are happy with your work environment or the attitude that you have toward work. The change of environment is necessary for you to observe yourself and assess how you have been dealing with work and life in general.

At this point, you may realize that you need to pay attention to your personal wellbeing, which involves your personal interests. The next chapter will show you how to make time for personal recreation.

Chapter 11 - How To Make Time For Your Hobbies

You probably have the feeling that you can never touch your favorite basketball again or have the time to update your stamp collection because you have been too busy at work. However, if you really love your personal activities, then having time for them should not be a problem. All you need to do is to find your free time.

Hobbies serve as your personal way of expressing yourself, and that also means spending time on them makes you feel like you have a life outside work. Your hobbies and interests also allow you to make yourself feel important and that your skills can be relevant even outside work.

The bigger problem is that if you have already forgotten what it is like to have a hobby, or to actually have personal time off. Face it – those years having that job may have made you abandon your leisurely games or made you a complete zombie with no interests. This chapter will help you not only find time for the things you like to do, but also remember that it is okay to have a hobby.

When You Do Not Know What You are Interested In

If you cannot think of anything to do during your free time, it may be wise to do the following:

1. Write down all the things you used to enjoy doing.

Imagine those years when you were free from obligation, not having to spend long hours tied to your cubicle. What were you doing back then? Did you love photography, or were you trying to learn how to play the guitar? Jot down all the activities you used to do all the time when you were younger.

Now, look at that list, and try to remember your favorite moments when you used to do those activities. Do you want to experience those fun times again? If so, then make the commitment to get that hobby back into your life.

2. Read interest articles.

If you know you were a huge fan of doodling, but you have not drawn anything lately, then rekindle the joy by reading stories of busy people being able to attend to their passion.

3. Join a club.

You may think that clubs are time-wasters, but you are wrong. Clubs are filled with busy people just like you trying to find time for their hobbies. Clubs are also a great way to force hobby time into your schedule. That way, you never have to tell yourself you do not have a free day for your personal activities.

Clubs do not necessarily propose a particular activity. They are also a great way to find people with similar lifestyles, and then learn the things they do for leisure. This also provides you with opportunity to widen your network and discover a hobby or two.

4. Take personality tests.

If you are unsure of what you want to do for leisure, then you may find a clue from taking personality tests. These tests give you an idea of what kind of activities you are probably interested in because of your lifestyle and predisposition toward life. If you are bored during your next break, go online and take these tests for free.

Make Your Work Hobby-Friendly

If you already know you have certain activities you want to do but cannot find the time to enjoy them, then you need to include them in your schedule. That means rearranging your work hours to accommodate activities that you find fun. Here are some life hacks that busy people should learn:

1. Bring your hobby to work.

As long as your hobby does not entail having to carry tons of equipment, then you should not have a problem doing this. If your hobbies are reading, taking photographs, or playing an instrument, you just need to find a space where no one can disturb you while you engage in these activities.

2. Take your meetings somewhere else.

If you are the one planning where to go for meetings, then it would probably be a good idea to go somewhere other than the conference room. You may squeeze in little moments of indulging in your leisure activities if the venue allows you to jam with the live band or take photographs, for example.

3. Use your commute time to plan your hobbies or to actually indulge in them.

Make travel less boring by bringing that book you have not read yet because work is eating up all your free time. You can also listen to the song you have been trying to learn the chords of. Take the idle time of commute to the next level by spending it thinking about the things you want to do during the next weekend.

Ensuring You Have Personal Time Off

Now that you know how to figure out what to do for yourself and you are anxious to see to it that your weekends would be free so you can do them, you need to find definite time to enjoy your hobbies. Doing that is simple – all you need to do is to treat them like scheduled activities.

1. Block off your schedule for your hobbies.

Make sure you allot a day or two for hobbies, which you can set as scheduled dates for prioritizing your other interests. Make sure you keep these dates free, and refrain from having to cancel your hobby schedule because of work.

2. Prioritize your activities

You may find that since you have hobby days in your week, you feel obliged to pay attention to all activities you are interested in. In order for you to actually enjoy those personal time-offs from work, see to it that you prioritize your leisure activities.

It may be a good idea to book a particular hobby for a month before you think about the other activities that you want to do. That way, you can more fully experience each activity.

3. Make it social.

One of the most effective ways of guaranteeing that you attend to your hobbies is to schedule them with your friends or loved ones in mind, or pay for a class. Not only does that make your activity more enjoyable, you also have the chance to meet other people that encourage you to take your hobbies more seriously.

4. Take 15 minutes off your tasks.

When you think about 15 minutes, you know it is a small amount of time just long enough for a power nap or a coffee break. When you are always pressed for time at work, 15 minutes can be enough for you to enjoy something personal. Since hobbies are typically activities that add up to your skills, you would realize that collectively, those 15 minutes you spent in a month can actually add up to enough time for you to learn something new, such as a new song to play on the guitar. When you look at this method, you can see there is no excuse to avoid enjoying personal time off.

Now that you know how to make time for your hobbies, you can learn how to never have a "buyer's remorse" when you enjoy personal time off. That means you can fruitfully enjoy your hobbies on days off. The next chapter will tell you more about that.

Chapter 12 - Budget Your Hobbies

Here is something that a lot of workaholics should acknowledge – taking a break from work and spending time for leisure, friends, or family is not a waste of time. However, most people who prefer to spend their time at work than with anything else have a very valid concern and that is money.

A lot of people think that the time they spend away from the office means having to spend a lot of money, and that defeats the entire purpose of working hard for savings. They do have a point – why spend your money for Caribbean cruises and overpriced hotel stays, when you can make more money and spend it for your children's college fund?

That entire idea can make you look away from leisure and bonding time with your loved ones and make your office cubicle more attractive. However, you have to understand that leisure and time off should not be viewed as things that only the rich can enjoy. When it comes to work/life balance, you can look at it from a very fair perspective, even when you involve economics. In order for you to feel you have the right to take a break, you have to find activities that suit your lifestyle and finances.

Still Aim for Better Things

That does not mean that people in the middle class do not have any right to dream about expensive vacations and gadgets. You just have to see to it that enjoying your personal time away from work does not mean going above the budget. By seeing to it that leisure is not beyond your means, you will more thoroughly enjoy your time outside of work.

Use Leisure as a Budgeting Tool

Among the best practices of people who enjoy work/life balance is that they use the fun things they do to measure their finances and see what other activities that they can do. It is also an important reminder that leisure may come with expenses, and it is very important to pay attention to them to know which activities you can afford.

For example, if you are into music and want to record a new song on your free time, you may have to think about buying recording gear or getting an instrument to use for recording. Without checking your budget for leisure, you may get dissuaded later on because you did not foresee that buying musical gear can be expensive. You could instead focus on writing the lyrics to the song you want to record, while you wait for the next payday to buy equipment. That way, you know you can afford home recording without having to sacrifice too much.

Enjoy Seasonal Hobbies by Booking in Advance

There are a lot of things you can do according to season, and it is wise to schedule time off accordingly. If you are on a budget and want to make the most of your free time and excess money, it would be a good idea to enjoy hobbies depending on what comes cheap during the season. For example, book farther in advance for discounted flight and hotel rates. Doing so prevents any hassle at work and saves you considerable amounts of money. It also gives you less reason to worry about what is happening at work while you are on a vacation.

At the same time, being able to foresee coming events that involve your interests would also grant you the ability to enjoy them in the most frugal manner. If you are into skiing, the best time to buy gear for that activity is during the off-season.

If you want to ensure you spend time and money wisely on your hobbies and see to it that they are not going to be in conflict with your obligations, all you need to do is have foresight. By planning and budgeting for your hobbies wisely, you realize there is nothing that stops you from doing what you want. You will also see that despite having a 9 to 5 job with overtime, you can create a lot of surplus time and money to enjoy personal activities.

Chapter 13 - Covering All Bases

When you think about having work/life balance now, you realize that it is not a myth but a necessary reality for you to achieve holistic growth. It also proves that while you want to make sure you tend to all your responsibilities, you are also ensuring you have the mental and physical capacity to be able to fulfill your obligations and that you are happy while doing so.

At the end, you should keep in mind that your happiness is your moral obligation and not just any ordinary personal achievement that you randomly wish to pursue. It should be your priority to fulfill this obligation to yourself and understand that being happy by achieving balance should not cost you anything.

Dealing With Worry and Guilt

If you feel that your job would be lost if you pay attention to your loved ones or your personal happiness in general, then you should probably examine if you are really happy with your job. If not, it would be a good idea to talk to your employer about specific work-related reforms. Keeping communication lines about this issue is very important, since every employer out there wants to ensure that his employees assume a lifestyle that helps them reach work goals. A reasonable employer would see to it that you have a workload that enables you to enjoy life as well.

Negotiate for Flexibility

If your work entails tasks beyond normal office hours, then you may want to ask your employer if there are options for flexibility, such as telecommuting instead of having to do everything in the office. If not, then consider talking about being able to delegate some of the tasks to your other teammates or having a more flexible time to fulfill tasks.

Remember That It is All About Planning

Being able to achieve work/life balance is all about being able to cover all bases and being able to manage time and other resources well. With proper negotiations in the workplace, being able to look at existing schedules and meeting deadlines efficiently, and prioritizing personal time, you can achieve harmony between personal life and work.

As long as you plan all your activities and you aim to avoid spreading yourself too thin, you will soon realize that this harmony can come naturally. You do not have to sweat it, actually – all you need to do is to give respect to your personal needs. Soon enough, you will realize that your work can give way for you to enjoy the best things in life.

Conclusion

Thank you again for purchasing this book!

I hope this book was able to help you to have an efficient system to perform well at work, while seeing to it that you have time for your family, friends and yourself. I also hope that this book has enabled you to get the most out of your week by having time for recreation and bonding with the most important people in your life.

The next step is to grab your planner and schedule all your activities for recreation and fun. Grab your phone and start booking your friends and family for some quality time. While you are at it, plan your next vacation as well.

Thank you and good luck!

Made in the USA
Lexington, KY
05 January 2015